Return to an Address of the Honorable the House of Con
dated 11 June 2009
for the

Report to the
Secretary of State
on the
Review of
Elective Home Education
in England

Graham Badman

Ordered by the House of Commons to be printed on
11 June 2009

HC 610   LONDON: THE STATIONERY OFFICE   £19.15

Institute of Education
University of London
20 Bedford Way
London
WC1H 0AL

Rt Hon Ed Balls MP
Secretary of State for Children, Schools and Families
Sanctuary Buildings
Great Smith Street
London
SW1P 3BT

Friday 29 May 2009

Dear Secretary of State

In January, you asked me to review the arrangements for home education in England. In particular, you asked me to look at whether there are any barriers to local authorities and other public agencies in effectively carrying out their safeguarding responsibilities in relation to home educated children. You also asked me to investigate suggestions that home education could be used as a 'cover' for child abuse. Finally, you asked me to look at whether local authorities are providing the right support to home educating families.

I enclose my report which I trust accurately reflects the wide variety of information provided to me over the course of the review.

As you will gather, I conclude that changes in the regulatory and legislative frameworks are necessary and I suggest in my report that you pursue this at the first available opportunity. I also conclude that home educating families should be better supported through improved access to services and facilities.

I hope you find the report useful.

Yours sincerely

Graham Badman CBE

Acknowledgments

I wish to thank all of the home educators and their children who extended to me the courtesy of explanation and who contributed to this report through questionnaire and letter.

I wish to thank also all of the local authority officers who did the same and my colleagues in the reference group for their advice and counsel.

But I wish to reserve special thanks and praise for Elizabeth Green of the DCSF who has worked tirelessly throughout this review with unfailing good humour. Without Elizabeth's advice, diligence and intellectual precision securing this report in the limited time available would simply not have been possible – she is a credit to the service.

G.M. Badman

Contents

" The need to choose, to sacrifice some ultimate values to others, turns out to be a permanent characteristic of the human predicament[1] "

ISAIAH BERLIN

1   Berlin, I (1969) *Four Essays on Liberty* London: Oxford University

1. Introduction

1.1   The review of elective home education, as the terms of reference (Annex A) make clear, has been triggered by a range of issues and representations, not least being the quite proper concern to ensure that systems for keeping children safe and ensuring that they receive a suitable education are as robust as possible.

1.2   During the course of the review I have been struck by the passion and commitment of many parents who either as a result of deeply held convictions or absolute necessity as they see it have chosen to educate their child or children at home. Indeed for many it is quite clear that this course of action is not without personal cost, often financial and professional. I have met some extraordinarily accomplished young people who have prospered as a consequence of elective home education of whom their parents are justly proud, but I am not persuaded that I could argue this to be a universal picture, any more than the same argument could be applied to the schooling system, but the same checks and balances do not apply.

1.3   I have read the many submissions made by home educators who argue their case from almost as many standpoints as there are children in elective home education – indeed to attempt to categorise the views of home educators or regard them as an homogenous group would simply be wrong. It is a cause of concern that although approximately 20,000 home educated children and young people are known to local authorities, estimates vary as to the real number which could be in excess of 80,000. I will discuss this later in this report. The degree of individualism exhibited may well be a strength but it militates against securing representative opinion and has led to factions within the elective home education community that actually distort the strength of philosophical commitment, achievement and need. I shall make recommendation in this regard.

1.4   I have taken account of the views of local authorities who are strongly of the opinion that the current guidelines are unworkable in that they are contradictory and confer responsibility without power. I agree with this view and will recommend accordingly. However, I also recognise that despite the excellent practice of some, there are local authorities who do not discharge their responsibilities properly, make effective use of current statutory powers or use the ingenuity referenced in the good practice illustrated later in this report. Good relationships and mutual respect are at the heart of the engagement of local authorities with home educating parents – this is evidenced in many authorities but such is the number of children now within elective home education that the development of these relationships cannot be left to chance or personality. The current disparity in practice across local authorities cannot continue – there is a need for a common national approach locally applied.

1.5   Few would argue with the assertion that parents are the prime educator within or outside of a schooling system. There is a considerable body of research evidence that points to this conclusion – parental attitude, support and expectation are the key determinants of educational success[2]. Indeed, as the national Children's Plan makes clear it is "*Parents not Government that bring up children*"[3] and there is nothing in this report which sets out to contradict or modify this contention. However, there has to be a balance between the rights of the parents and the rights of the child. I believe that balance is not achieved through current legislation or guidance, and the imbalance must be addressed. Not to do so could result in the concerns for a minority being applied to the vast majority of caring, motivated home educating parents.

---

2   See for example, Desforges, C & Abouchaar, A (2003) *The Impact of Parental Involvement, Parental Support and Family Education on Pupil Achievement and Adjustment: A Literature Review*, London, Department for Education and Skills, Research Report No 433.
3   *The Children's Plan*, DCSF, 2007, CM7280

2. Conduct of the Review

2.1   The terms of reference stated the scope of the review was to be limited to practice in England.

2.2   The review was conducted by means of structured interview with a range of stakeholders including home educating parents and children, visits to local authorities and home education groups, a public call for evidence and a questionnaire to all top tier local authorities in England. Over two thousand responses to the call for evidence were received, more than three quarters of which were from home educating parents or children. Ninety responses to the local authority questionnaire were received, which equates to a 60% response rate.

2.3   The review was further informed by a literature review and consideration of practice and legislation in other countries. A list of the organisations and local authorities I consulted and from whom I took evidence is at Annex B. A copy of the questionnaire used in the public call for evidence is at Annex C. A copy of the questionnaire to local authorities is at Annex D.

3. Current Legislation and Regulation

3.1   As my introductory comments make clear, I am not persuaded that under the current regulatory regime[4] that there is a correct balance between the rights of parents and the rights of the child either to an appropriate education or to be safe from harm. That being said I am not in anyway arguing that elective home education is intrinsically wrong or that within the elective home education community there is not exemplary practice. Indeed, there is a strong argument to commission further research to better inform understanding of "personalisation" as an element of student progression and achievement. I shall return to this issue later.

3.2   The question is simply a matter of balance and securing the right regulatory regime within a framework of legislation that protects the rights of all children, even if in transaction such regulation is only necessary to protect a minority.

3.3   The United Nations Convention on the Rights of the Child (UNCRC) gives children and young people over forty substantive rights which include the right to express their views freely, the right to be heard in any legal or administrative matters that affect them and the right to seek, receive and impart information and ideas. Article 12 makes clear the responsibility of signatories to give children a voice:

> *"Parties shall assure to the child who is capable of forming his or her own views the right to express those views freely in all matters affecting the child, the views of the child being given due weight in accordance with the age and maturity of the child."*

Yet under the current legislation and guidance, local authorities have no right of access to the child to determine or ascertain such views.

3.4   Furthermore Article 28 of the UNCRC recognises the right of the child to an education. Education is compulsory in England and it can be provided at school *"or otherwise"*[5]. The responsibility for the provision of a child's education rests with their parents who also have a duty to ensure that any education provided is "efficient", "full time" and "suitable". This is set out in Section 7 of the Education Act 1996 which provides that:

---

4   The current legislative and regulatory framework is outlined at Annex E.
5   Section 7 Education Act 1996

> *"The parent of every child of compulsory school age shall cause him to receive efficient full-time education suitable –*
> *(a) to his age, ability and aptitude, and*
> *(b) to any special educational needs he may have, either by regular attendance at school or otherwise."*

3.5   The terms "efficient" and "suitable" education are not defined in law, despite the detailed prescription of expectations in schools. Case law[6] has broadly described an "efficient" education as one that "achieves that which it sets out to achieve". A "suitable" education is one that:

> *"primarily equips a child for life within the community of which he is a member, rather than the way of life in the country as a whole, as long as it does not foreclose the child's options in later years to adopt some other form of life if he wishes to do so".*

3.6   This poses a further problem for local authorities charged with a statutory duty under section 437 (1) Education Act 1996 in that they are required to intervene:

> *"If it appears to a local education authority that a child of compulsory school age in their area is not receiving suitable education, either by regular attendance at school or otherwise, they shall serve a notice in writing on the parent requiring him to satisfy them within the period specified in the notice that the child is receiving such education".*

Additionally local authorities have a duty[7] which requires them to:

> *..... make arrangements to enable them to establish (so far as it is possible to do so) the identities of children in their area who are of compulsory school age but—*
> *(a) are not registered pupils at a school, and*
> *(b) are not receiving suitable education otherwise than at a school.*

---

6   Mr Justice Woolf in the case of R v Secretary of State for Education and Science, ex parte Talmud Torah Machzikei Hadass School Trust (12 April 1985)

7   Section 436A Education Act 1996 inserted by section 4(1) Education and Inspections Act 2006

3.7 Within current guidance local authorities are *"encouraged to address the situation informally"*[8]. Such an approach may or may not be sufficient. How can local authorities know what they don't know with no means of determining the number of children who are being electively home educated in their area, or the quality of what is provided, without rights of access to the child? For many, perhaps the majority of home educating families, this approach may be sufficient. However, I do not believe that such arrangements are sufficiently robust to protect the rights of all children.

3.8 The European Convention on Human Rights (ECHR) Article 2 of Protocol 1 states:

> *"No person shall be denied the right to education. In the exercise of any functions which it assumes in relation to education and to teaching, the State shall respect the right of parents to ensure such education and teaching is in conformity with their own religious and philosophical convictions."*

3.9 This Article is much quoted by home educators in defence of their rights as parents to educate their children as they see fit. However, case law on the ECHR challenges any claim that home education is a fundamental right:

> *"The second sentence of Article 2 [of Protocol 1] must however be read together with the first which enshrines the right of everyone to education. It is on to this fundamental right that is grafted the right of parents to respect for their religious and philosophical convictions. ...Furthermore, respect is only due to convictions on the part of the parents which do not conflict with the fundamental right of the child to education"*[9]

And:

> *"The Commission notes that the first sentence of Article 2 of Protocol No 1 .. enshrines the fundamental right of the child to education. This right by its very nature calls for regulation by the State, regulation which may vary in time and place according to the needs and resources of the community and of individuals."*[10]

---

8 Department for Children, Schools and Families. *Elective Home Education Guidelines for Local Authorities* (HMSO, 2007)
9 B.N and S.N v Sweden no 17678/91
10 Leuffen v Germany no 19844/92

3.10   In addition, in one exchange of emails during the course of this review one parent, in arguing the case for the freedom of home education, cited the words of A.S. Neill:

> *"The function of the child is to live his own life – not the life that his anxious parents think he should live, nor a life according to the purpose of the educator who thinks he knows best."*[11]

This quotation could equally well be applied to home educating parents as to the schooling system that A.S. Neill challenged with the curriculum and methodology of Summerhill School.

3.11   This review does not argue against the rights of parents as set out in Section 7 of the Education Act 1996 outlined above, nor their deeply held convictions about education. I believe it would be wrong to seek to legislate in pursuit of an all embracing definition of "suitable". However, such is the demand and complexity of 21st Century society and employment that further thought should be given to what constitutes an appropriate curriculum within the context of elective home education. Such a curriculum must be sufficiently broad and balanced and relevant to enable young people to make suitable choices about their life and likely future employment. Article 29 of the UNCRC states that:

> *"State Parties agree that the education of the child shall be directed to:*
> *(a)   The development of the child's personality, talents and mental and physical abilities to their fullest potential;*
> *(b)   The development of respect for human rights and fundamental freedoms, and for the principles enshrined in the Charter of the United Nations;*
> *(c)   The development of respect for the child's parents, his or her own cultural identity, language and values, for the national values of the country in which the child is living, the country from which he or she may originate, and for civilizations different from his or her own;*
> *(d)   The preparation of the child for responsible life in a free society, in the spirit of understanding, peace, tolerance, equality of sexes, and friendship among all peoples, ethnic, national and religious groups and persons of indigenous origin;*
> *(e)   The development of respect for the natural environment."*

It could be argued that adherence to Article 29 would demand further definition of the term "efficient".

---

11   Neill, A.S. (1960), *Summerhill: A Radical Approach to Child Rearing*, New York, NY: Hart

3.12　As stated previously, the term "efficient" has been described in case law as an education that *"achieves that which it sets out to achieve"*. On this basis there surely can be no argument against those who choose to educate their children at home being required to articulate their educational approach or 'philosophy', intentions and practice and with their child demonstrate its effectiveness. Indeed many do so already. This is not an argument for prescription; on the contrary it is simply an argument that the rights of parents are equally matched by the rights of the child and a recognition of the moral imperative of securing education for all children commensurate with their age, aptitude, ability and any special needs.

In the light of the above I therefore make the following recommendations:

RECOMMENDATION 1

That the DCSF establishes a compulsory national registration scheme, locally administered, for all children of statutory school age, who are, or become, electively home educated.

- **This scheme should be common to all local authorities.**
- **Registration should be renewed annually.**
- **Those who are registering for the first time should be visited by the appropriate local authority officer within one month of registration.**
- **Local authorities should ensure that all home educated children and young people already known to them are registered on the new scheme within one month of its inception and visited over the following twelve months, following the commencement of any new legislation.**
- **Provision should be made to allow registration at a local school, children's centre or other public building as determined by the local authority.**
- **When parents are thinking of deregistering their child/children from school to home educate, schools should retain such pupils on roll for a period of 20 school days so that should there be a change in circumstances, the child could be readmitted to the school. This period would also allow for the resolution of such difficulties that may have prompted the decision to remove the child from school.**
- **National guidance should be issued on the requirements of registration and be made available online and at appropriate public buildings. Such guidance must**

include a clear statement of the statutory basis of elective home education and the rights and responsibilities of parents.

■ At the time of registration parents/carers/guardians must provide a clear statement of their educational approach, intent and desired/planned outcomes for the child over the following twelve months.

■ Guidance should be issued to support parents in this task with an opportunity to meet local authority officers to discuss the planned approach to home education and develop the plan before it is finalised. The plan should be finalised within eight weeks of first registration.

■ As well as written guidance, support should encompass advice from a range of advisers and organisations, including schools. Schools should regard this support as a part of their commitment to extended schooling.

■ Where a child is removed from a school roll to be home educated, the school must provide to the appropriate officer of the local authority a record of the child's achievement to date and expected achievement, within 20 school days of the registration, together with any other school records.

■ Local authorities must ensure that there are mechanisms/systems in place to record and review registrations annually.

RECOMMENDATION 2

That the DCSF review the current statutory definition of what constitutes a "suitable" and "efficient" education in the light of the Rose review of the primary curriculum, and other changes to curriculum assessment and definition throughout statutory school age. Such a review should take account of the five Every Child Matters outcomes determined by the 2004 Children Act, should not be overly prescriptive but be sufficiently defined to secure a broad, balanced, relevant and differentiated curriculum that would allow children and young people educated at home to have sufficient information to enable them to expand their talents and make choices about likely careers. The outcome of this review should further inform guidance on registration.

Home educators should be engaged in this process.

4. Elective Home Education in Context – the Views of Home Educators and Others

4.1   At the risk of stating the obvious, in seeking evidence as to how the current system operates it begs the question – what system? The differing approaches of local authorities and extraordinary range of practice amongst home educators defy simple categorisation. Indeed, one of the major concerns of home educators within the current system was the inability of some local authority officers to appreciate and understand their practice. I shall return to the role and remit of local authorities in a later section, but I believe it is important to try to capture the views of the many home educators who contributed to this review.

4.2   In the main, home educators in their responses through questionnaire, email, letter and interview were fiercely defensive of their rights and actions. There were some who welcomed the visits of local authority officers and the support offered through drop-in centres, resources and materials and some argued for more regularised monitoring and intervention. However, there were those who wanted nothing from the local authority nor any contact with it.

4.3   The range of response principally outside the public call for evidence varied enormously from:

> "...no one from the LA [local authority] would in my opinion be on my child's intellectual level or they wouldn't be working for the LA."

to the more measured:

> "I would be happy to discuss my children's education with my local authority, but would expect the LA representative to have a good understanding of the law relating to EHE [elective home education], the principles underpinning the law, how children learn and in our case, special educational needs".

4.4   To the above could have been added literally dozens of other quotations. They constitute a heady mixture of pent up rage, frustration, resentment and a rejection of third party judgement. In seeking to understand such responses it is important to examine the reasons why elective home education was chosen by parents in the first place. A study commissioned by the then Department for Education and Skills (DfES) in 2007 concluded:

> *"Reasons for home education vary and the decision to home educate is often due to a combination of factors that may be subject to change over time. Common reasons cited for opting to home educate include bullying, discontentment with the quality of education provided in school, or parents' religious, cultural and ideological beliefs. Risk of prosecution for non-attendance and inadequate provision for special educational needs are increasingly cited as reasons to educate according to some local authorities."[12]*

These findings are endorsed by a small scale research project by the National Foundation for Educational Research (2006)[13] which placed further emphasis on parents disillusionment with schools and their inability to meet their child's needs as they saw them.

4.5   My own conversations with individuals and groups of home educating parents would confirm the above with the addition of a significant number who chose this route for ideological and philosophical reasons or simply because they believe they "can do it better".

4.6   Whatever the reasons, I believe it is important for local authorities both to analyse and consider why an increasing number of parents are choosing elective home education both for the betterment of children services as a whole and the monitoring and support of electively home educated children.

RECOMMENDATION 3

That all local authorities analyse the reasons why parents or carers chose elective home education and report those findings to the Children's Trust Board, ensuring that this analysis contributes to the debate that determines the Children and Young People's Plan.

4.7   There were, of course, some contrary views to those summarised above, from local authorities (considered later) and others. The National Association of Schoolmasters/Union of Women Teachers (NASUWT) in its response to the call for evidence, was quite clear in its opposition to the whole basis of elective home education as currently defined:

---

12 Hopwood,V.,O'Neill, L., Castro G. & Hodgson, B. (2007) *The Prevalence of Home Education in England: A Feasibility Study*, DfES, Research Report 827
13 Kendall S. & Atkinson, M (2006) *Some perspectives on home educated children,* NFER

> *"The NASUWT maintains the existence of a right to home educate is anomalous with the clear emphasis in Government policy of ensuring that all children and young people can benefit from educational provision where teaching and learning is led by qualified teachers in well resourced and fit for purpose modern educational settings."*

4.8   The Association of School and College Leaders (ASCL) does not go as far in its argument but raises fears about ensuring a system that does not harm children. The British Humanist Association raised concerns in their submission to the review as follows:

> *"some of those who choose to educate their children at home for religious reasons may not be providing schooling that is adequate, either according to the Every Child Matters agenda or the principles of Article 29 of the UN Convention on the Rights of the Child".*

And the Education Division of the Church of England states its concern:

> *"that children and young people not in formal education are missing the benefits and challenges of learning in community with their peers. Children who do not go to school may not experience the social and cultural diversity encountered there; they will not learn how to deal with the rough and tumble of everyday life; they may never meet people with different faith and value systems. All such encounters, even the difficult or painful ones are enriching. We are concerned not only with the five Every Child Matters outcomes, but also with the spiritual well-being of all children and young people. Spiritual well-being arises not only from being cared for in a loving family and/or faith community, but also in encounters with people of different opinions and backgrounds; in learning to listen to a variety of opinions; to encounter diversity and the riches and life-enhancement it can bring. Spiritual well-being depends on living and taking a full part in community life. Children and young people in schools learn about and from the five major religions. This may be a difficult part of the curriculum for home educators to provide, yet it is vital for the Government's community cohesion agenda that all children learn in a balanced way about the variety of religious values and practices, and to be encouraged to question their own beliefs and practices."*

4.9   In addition there were of course detailed responses from elective home education organisations (see Annex B) which have proved invaluable in the course of this inquiry.

'Education Otherwise', a home education group, in a detailed set of proposals, listed recommendations they would wish to see as a consequence of the review. However, this evidence apart, what I believe to be of significance was that the immediate response of many other home educators was to disown any such series of proposals and distance themselves from the arguments put forward.

4.10   Herein I believe lies a fundamental problem, namely the absence of a representative voice for home educating parents and home educated children. The Government of Tasmania supports a system that not only gives elective home educators a voice in policy determination but also a role in the monitoring and support of other home educating families. Having raised this notion with both groups of home educators and individuals, such a structure at this time may be a step too far but I do believe there is need for a representative body at a local level so that there is a regular exchange of views and transfer of knowledge between local authority and home educating parents and children. I do not underestimate the difficulty of creating such a representative body but believe it to be essential if the recommendations in this report are to be effective in giving greater assurance to the state about the wellbeing and education of a significant number of children, and affording the freedom to educate their children that many parents have sought. If nothing else such a body should promote understanding and bring about the dissemination of good practice.

RECOMMENDATION 4

That the local authority should establish a Consultative Forum for home educating parents to secure their views and representative opinion. Such a body could be constituted as a sub-group of the Children's Trust with a role in supporting the development of the Children's Trust, and the intentions of the local authority with regard to elective home education.

5. The Current and Future Role of Local Authorities and Children's Trusts

5.1 As outlined in the previous section, local authorities were much criticised by home educators in their responses to this review, for their perceived lack of understanding of the various methodologies and approaches within home education and their manner of engagement with the parent and/or child. On the other hand, local authorities often expressed considerable anxiety for the wellbeing and progress of some children and the failure of some parents to respond to what they regarded were quite legitimate requests for information about the suitability of education. They have expressed in response to questionnaire and in interview their dissatisfaction with the current legislative position and guidance, which many find unworkable. In particular, the absence of a more precise definition of what constitutes a "suitable" and "efficient" education militates against benchmarked attainment and being denied access to the place of education, and the opportunity to speak with the child, prevents them from fulfilling their current statutory duties referred to previously.

5.2 That said, I have been greatly impressed in my visits and conversations with local authorities by what has been achieved through partnership and the fostering of good relationships. Partnership not just with home educating parents and children but also with other agencies. This partnership approach strengthens the local authority's support to home educators and increases their knowledge of the progress and wellbeing of the child or children.

The following case studies demonstrate the commitment and ingenuity of local authorities. This list is by no means exhaustive. Implicit within the following examples is the importance of mutual respect, regular information and the celebration of the achievements of many home educated children.

> **North Yorkshire County Council** organises a regular 'drop-in day' whereby home educating parents and children can meet each other as well as professionals from the local authority who can discuss issues, ask advice, share resources and discuss plans for the future direction of education, such as routes into college or university. It is also a 'fun day' with interactive sessions such as 'brain profiling' or simply playing computer games. Crucially, parents and children are asked to complete an evaluation form to feedback what they liked and didn't like and what they'd like to see at the next session.

Staffordshire County Council, like many local authorities, publish a booklet for home educating families which provides clear information in 'parent friendly' language to all parents thinking about home educating their child/ren. It clearly sets out the legal requirements including the rights and responsibilities of parents and the role of the local authority. It also prompts parents into considering what home education entails whilst also offering them support, a list of useful resources and contacts with local home education groups. The overall tone of the information is supportive, respectful and demonstrates a clear understanding of the law and also the variation within home education. The material also clearly provides the name and contact details of the local authority officer leading on elective home education within the authority as well as details of complaints procedures.

Somerset County Council ensures there is effective and ongoing contact with the local Connexions service for all electively home educated youngsters aged 13 to 16. It ensures that Connexions are in contact with electively home educated young people and that appropriate support is offered. The County Council have worked extensively with the local home education community and further education establishments to secure better access for electively home educated young people to both vocational and academic courses. Somerset has also offered to pay for examination entry and administration fees for individual home educated students who have been registered with the local authority for two years leading up to the examination. This arrangement will be agreed on an individual basis with an Elective Home Education Officer. Somerset has offered workshops to home educating families on literacy, numeracy and storytelling. They have also run a residential experience at a local activity centre for Year 5, 6 and 7 pupils on their elective home education register for the last two years, and a third residential is planned for this September.

West Midlands local authorities' regional home education forum
The purpose of these termly meetings, convened by a local authority in the West Midlands, is to provide participating authorities with a forum to discuss and debate common issues and concerns that are either of a local, regional or national interest. A further key objective is to strengthen authorities' understanding and shape consistent practice/delivery. Representatives from home education groups are invited and this interaction with the home education community is seen as crucial in helping to build mutual respect and break down barriers and misconceptions.

The above exemplifications of good practice are in total accord with the demands and recommendations of The Children's Plan and fit well with the developments of Children's Trusts. However such practice must not be left to chance.

RECOMMENDATION 5

That the DCSF should bring forward proposals requiring all local authorities to report to the Children's Trust Board making clear how it intends to monitor and support children and young people being educated at home, in accord with Recommendation 1.

5.3   Furthermore in accord with Recommendation 5 above, given the variety and complexity of elective home education, I recommend:

RECOMMENDATION 6

That local authorities should, where appropriate, commission the monitoring and support of home education through the local Children's Trust Board, thereby securing a multidisciplinary approach and the likely use of expertise from other agencies and organisations, including the voluntary sector.

5.4   To properly exercise the functions listed above and given that requirements of registration detailed in Recommendation 1, I believe that further changes in regulation are required:

RECOMMENDATION 7

The DCSF should bring forward proposals to change the current regulatory and statutory basis to ensure that in monitoring the efficiency and suitability of elective home education:

- That designated local authority officers should:

  - have the right of access to the home;
  - have the right to speak with each child alone if deemed appropriate or, if a child is particularly vulnerable or has particular communication needs, in the company of a trusted person who is not the home educator or the parent/carer.

In so doing, officers will be able to satisfy themselves that the child is safe and well.

- That a requirement is placed upon local authorities to secure the monitoring of the effectiveness of elective home education as determined in Recommendation 1.

- That parents be required to allow the child through exhibition or other means to demonstrate both attainment and progress in accord with the statement of intent lodged at the time of registration.

5.5 Such new powers will still depend upon, and be more effective, where there are good relationships and mutual trust, respect and open communication between the home educating family and the local authority. The home may well become the place of education but it is first and foremost a home and many home educators maintain that given the nature of elective home education it is impossible to separate education from the normal, everyday life of the family. This contention is supported by the research of Jane Lowe and Alan Thomas[14] and one that I accept absolutely. I therefore recommend, contingent on the acceptance of this report, that within revised guidelines:

RECOMMENDATION 8

That reasonable warning of intended visit and invitation to exhibit should be given to home educators, parents and carers, not less than two weeks in advance. A written report of each visit must be filed within 21 days and copied to the home educating parent and child. A suitable process for factual correction and challenge to the content must be in place and made known to all parties.

5.6 Developing this new regime of monitoring and support will not be easy and will require a range of skills and understanding. The commissioning of services through the Children's Trust

---

14 Lowe, J. & Thomas, A. (2002) *Educating your Child at Home,* London

will bring new professional disciplines to bear in some cases and crucially, bring about third sector engagement, particularly in support of home educated children and young people who have special educational needs. Nevertheless training will be necessary not least to dispel the firmly held conviction amongst many home educators that current monitoring arrangements are too often framed from a schooling perspective.

RECOMMENDATION 9

That all local authority officers and others engaged in the monitoring and support of elective home education must be suitably trained. This training must include awareness of safeguarding issues and a full understanding of the essential difference, variation and diversity in home education practice, as compared to schools. Wherever possible and appropriate, representatives of the home educating community should be involved in the development and/or provision of such training. It is recommended that all officers be trained in the use of the Common Assessment Framework.

5.7   The good practice referred to earlier is illustrative of the attempts of many authorities to extend a range of opportunities to young people educated at home but again the picture is not universal. Many home educating parents, for reasons outlined earlier, having rejected the schooling system, do not re-engage for fear of further requirements or restrictions, yet they remain tax payers who contribute to the education system in the normal way. Many simply accept that "that's the way it is" but it seems to me perverse to articulate concern about thousands of young people yet cut them off from services that would be rightfully theirs if they attended school. I shall return to this issue in the final section of this report. In the responses from home educating parents, there was no overall consensus as to the support they would like or seek but there was almost universal support for free access to the public examination system. I believe this to be fair and arguably a natural extension of the state's desire to secure appropriate outcomes for young people.

RECOMMENDATION 10

That all local authorities should offer a menu of support to home educating families in accord with the requirements placed upon them by the power of wellbeing, extended schools and community engagement and other legislation. To that end local authorities must provide support for home educating children and young people to find appropriate examination centres and provide entries free to all home educated candidates who have demonstrated sufficiently their preparedness through routine monitoring, for all DCSF funded qualifications.

RECOMMENDATION 11

That in addition to Recommendation 10 above, local authorities should, in collaboration with schools and colleges:

- Extend and make available the opportunities of flexi-schooling.
- Extend access to school libraries, sports facilities, school visits, specialist facilities and key stage assessment.
- Provide access to specialist music tuition on the same cost basis.
- Provide access to work experience.
- Provide access to post 14 vocational opportunities.
- Signpost to third sector support where they have specialist experience and knowledge, for example, provision for bullied children.

5.8   I wish also to give some consideration to the impact and availability of information and communication technology (ICT) to home educated children and young people. This could be a report in itself but suffice it to say that the importance of ICT in learning, access to knowledge and information, communication and employment is self evident. Many home educating families, perhaps the majority, already make good use of the national infrastructure to support their child's education as well as facilities for networking within home educating community. Nevertheless, I believe it is important to add to the menu of opportunities and suggestions listed above so that every effort is made to prevent a home educated child being in any way disadvantaged. I therefore recommend that:

RECOMMENDATION 12

- BECTA considers the needs of the home educating community in the national roll out of the home access initiative.
- That local authorities consider what support and access to ICT facilities could be given to home educated children and young people through the existing school networks and the use of school based materials.
- That the QCA should consider the use of ICT in the testing and exam process with regard to its impact on home educated children and young people.

5.9   As I trust the foregoing makes clear, I believe that local authorities have a vital role in supporting elective home education and by so doing, assuring themselves of the attainments of the many young people so educated. From my analysis of their responses, visits and discussions I am confident of their ability to rise to the challenges implicit within this report. Nevertheless in pursuit of more uniform provision and action I recommend the following:

RECOMMENDATION 13

That local authority provision in regard to elective home education is brought into the scope of Ofsted's assessment of children's services within the Comprehensive Area Assessment through information included in the National Indicator Set (Recommendation 25), the annual Local Safeguarding Children Board report (Recommendation 21) and any other relevant information available to inspectors.

6. The Number of Electively Home Educated Children

6.1   It is a matter of some concern that despite a number of research studies and reports, it was not possible to identify with any degree of accuracy the number of children and young people currently educated at home. Our own data concurred with the DfES (2007) report, that there are around 20,000 children and young people currently registered with local authorities. We know that to be an underestimate and agree it is likely to be double that figure, if not more, possibly up to 80,000 children. I have no doubt that the vast majority of these children and young people are safe and well but, that may not be true for all.

6.2   ContactPoint will record the place where a child is being educated, where that is known, including where a child is being educated at home.[15]

6.3   Registration proposed within this report should complete the picture and offer further evidence of their wellbeing and educational progress. This information will complement the duty on local authorities to identify children not receiving a suitable education[16]. But because of the importance to local authorities of knowing the number of children and young people within the elective home education cohort, to assist in their commissioning of school places and to their understanding of why children were withdrawn from school, I believe it is important to report such information to the Children's Trust, together with data concerning their use of current statutory orders, whether to supervise education or direct attendance at school.

RECOMMENDATION 14

That the DCSF require all local authorities to make an annual return to the Children's Trust Board regarding the number of electively home educated children and young people and the number of School Attendance Orders and Education Supervision Orders as defined in the 1996 Education Act, issued to home educated children and young people.

6.4   While home education may sometimes be considered to be a better option for some children than mainstream education, parents should never be placed under pressure by schools to remove their children from school under threat of permanent exclusion or prosecution. I have heard evidence to this effect. The first priority of schools should always be to discuss with

---

15 Further information on ContactPoint is at: http://www.everychildmatters.gov.uk/contactpoint
16 *Revised statutory guidance for local authorities in England to identify children not receiving a suitable education*, DCSF, January 2009

parents what support can be provided to keep their child in school and to ensure they behave well and attend regularly.

RECOMMENDATION 15

That the DCSF take such action as necessary to prevent schools or local authorities advising parents to consider home education to prevent permanent exclusion or using such a mechanism to deal with educational or behavioural issues.

6.5 There are some electively home educated children and young people who may wish to return to school. Many home educated young people do return to school or college, a number post 16 or earlier, to pursue vocational or academic courses. However, local authorities have advised that such a return is sometimes a problem, particularly if the only school place available is at a school where the child was previously registered. For a small minority I believe it is important to give local authorities powers in common with those held for looked after children to direct beyond planned admission numbers. Such powers must not of course be used simply to avoid the normal admission arrangements and local authorities would clearly only use this discretionary power when it was absolutely clear that the needs of the child or young person could not be met otherwise.

RECOMMENDATION 16

That the DCSF bring forward proposals to give local authorities power of direction with regard to school places for children and young people returning to school from home education above planned admission limits in circumstances where it is quite clear that the needs of the child or young person could not be met without this direction.

7. Special Educational Needs

7.1   In formulating a response to the evidence submitted to this inquiry I have tried to retain in the forefront of my mind the particular issues that relate to those young people educated at home with special educational needs (SEN). For although as a group they simply form part of the cohort of those educated at home and should be covered by the generality of regulation, I am quite clear that their support and monitoring from local authorities or other agencies should be significantly different. The evidence offered is punctuated by very convincing case studies of hardship, anxiety and misunderstanding that would confirm the research evidence that many parents whose children have needs as diverse as dyslexia and autism, withdrew their child often in despair that their needs were not being adequately met in school. In such instances, it is often a case of 'home education by default' rather than 'elective home education'

7.2   Evidence submitted to this review by the National Autistic Society, Autism in Mind and particularly the Independent Panel for Special Educational Advice (IPSEA), all raise searching questions about the quality of support that follows a child into elective home education, and the methodology by which that support is offered. Similar points are made by individual parents, some of whom seek no help from the local authority even when their child has a statement of special educational needs. Many point to the need for greater sensitivity in intervention, indeed some are fearful that the act of monitoring would in itself be damaging to the child.

7.3   IPSEA, in its submission to this review, cite a range of reasons why children with special educational needs become educated at home:

> *"...some families with children with SEN make a positive choice to educate their children at home. For others it is the least bad option which may come about for a number of reasons:*
>
> - *Inadequacy of local SEN provision e.g. lack of special schools or lack of appropriately resourced units in mainstream schools*
> - *School or LA failure to make statemented provision*
> - *Breakdown of relationships with school &/or LA*
> - *Withdrawal as an act of desperation in the interests of the child's mental or physical well-being e.g. when he/she is being badly bullied*
> - *Being asked to leave/exclusion by a school which cannot cope with the extreme behaviour linked with the child's disability*
> - *Neutral position pending tribunal hearing (e.g. on secondary transfer)*
> - *Response to unsuccessful tribunal*
> - *Religious reasons e.g. lack of local school of relevant faith which can cater for SEN child*
> - *Response to threats of prosecution when a child is out of school for reasons above*
>
> *It is clearly a matter of grave concern that some of the most vulnerable children including those with very complex special needs, should end up out of school through a default in the system. Once a child is being home educated, Local Authorities may decline to provide support or make special educational provision. This is a situation which IPSEA commonly encounters."*

7.4   They also express concern about the amount of time a child may be 'in limbo' awaiting a new assessment or out of school pending a First-Tier Tribunal (Special Educational Needs and Disability). Almost all of the evidence submitted to the review around special needs points to the need for constructive relationships and adequate training of local authority staff. In line with the approach outlined in Recommendation 6, local authorities could commission new, independent experts and existing third sector organisations to support and monitor children with special educational needs who are educated at home, and meet the proposed duty of the local authority to monitor the elective home education, and in some cases, the statement of SEN. IPSEA endorse this approach.

More work needs to be done in this area and I therefore recommend:

RECOMMENDATION 17

That the Ofsted review of SEN provision give due consideration to home educated children with special educational needs and make specific reference to the support of those children.

7.5   That being said I also believe that immediate action should be taken both to regularise the current position, ensure that local authorities meet their obligation to monitor statements of special educational needs and secure adequate resources and support for the child. To that end I recommend:

RECOMMENDATION 18

That the DCSF should reinforce in guidance to local authorities the requirement to exercise their statutory duty to assure themselves that education is suitable and meets the child's special educational needs. They should regard the move to home education as a trigger to conduct a review and satisfy themselves that the potentially changed complexity of education provided at home, still constitutes a suitable education. The statement should then be revised accordingly to set out that the parent has made their own arrangements under section 7 of the Education Act 1996.

In the wake of the Ofsted review, changes to the SEN framework and legislation may be required.

RECOMMENDATION 19

That the statutory review of statements of SEN in accord with Recommendation 18 above be considered as fulfilling the function of mandatory annual review of elective home education recommended previously.

RECOMMENDATION 20

When a child or young person without a statement of special educational needs has been in receipt of School Action Plus support, local authorities and other agencies should give due consideration to whether that support should continue once the child is educated at home – irrespective of whether or not such consideration requires a new commissioning of service.

7.6 Local authorities should also pay particular attention to the Lamb Inquiry[17] comments relating to partnership with parents and the need for transparency in communication[18]. In the same inquiry, comments made regarding better and more communication with parents[19] could equally well be applied to the expectation parents should have of local authorities when they elect to home educate.

---

17 Lamb Inquiry Review of SEN and Disability Information; Brian Lamb; April 29th 2009 HTU www.dcsf.gov.uk/lambinquiry/.
18 Ibid p 7, para 27
19 Ibid p6, para 24

8. Safeguarding

8.1   Of all the matters considered during the course of this inquiry the question of safeguarding electively home educated children has prompted the most vociferous response. Many parents have expressed anger and outrage that it was suggested that elective home education could be used as a cover for abuse. They have not been slow to point out that the most dangerous and damaging abuse of children is often before statutory school age or where children have been withdrawn from school or are already known to children's social care.

8.2   Many home educators argue that press coverage of this review has cast them as "guilty" with a need to prove "innocence" just by virtue of being a home educator. And many have argued for a measured response to prevent "hard cases becoming bad law". In addressing this issue I have tried to answer two fundamental questions:

- First, if there is abuse of children within the home education community, is it disproportionally high, relative to the general population?

- Secondly where abuse does exist, would a change of regulation with regard to elective home education have either prevented or ameliorated such abuse?

8.3   It would be wrong to assume that home educators do not take the question of child safety, their own and others, very seriously. Some home educators who contributed to this review argued for periodic spot checks by authorities. The view was also expressed that attendance at school was no guarantee of a child's safety, as other tragic cases have indicated.

8.4   I understand the argument but do not accept it in its entirety in that attendance at school brings other eyes to bear, and does provide opportunity for the child to disclose to a trusted adult. Furthermore the 2004 Children Act, with its emphasis upon five outcomes for children including their safety not just their achievement, places new responsibilities upon schools to work with other agencies in a preventative way.

8.5   Some home educators have access to support and guidance from their organisations on recognising and dealing with child protection and many in conversation stressed to me the importance of their informal networks and knowledge of their own community. I am not persuaded that, although laudable, this is sufficient. Apart from which, on the basis of local authority responses to my questionnaire, there are many children likely to be unknown to the authorities or engaged in such networks. The process of registration recommended earlier should address this issue.

8.6   In seeking to answer the two questions posed earlier I have sought evidence and advice from protecting services and a range of third sector and other agencies that are engaged in the promotion of child safety and the protection of children. I have also analysed recent serious case reviews and sought information from local authorities on the number of electively home educated children subject to a child protection plan or were previously on the Child Protection Register.

The NSPCC is quite clear in its response in seeking a registration scheme and changed guidance.[20]

> "We do not agree that the status quo should be maintained and do think that monitoring should be strengthened. We are concerned that the child's safety and welfare should be paramount and that there is nothing in the current guidance or framework that would prevent children from being abused by people who may claim to be home educators. The current guidance on EHE [elective home education] says that the local authority can investigate if they have a concern about the child's education, but they do not have the powers to visit or meet the child. The guidance (paragraph 2.15) refers to the ability to see a child under s47 of the Children Act 1989. In order for a professional to use s47 they "must have reasonable cause to suspect that a child who lives or is found, in their area is suffering, or likely to suffer, significant harm". If a child who is being abused is not afforded opportunities outwith the house, then the slim chances of them being identified become even smaller than they already are. In such a situation, because there is no education concern, the local authority does not investigate, as there are no grounds to do so. If a member of the public sees the child (and this would need to be regularly) then they are unlikely to contact an appropriate body. It then becomes a catch 22 as no concern is raised, because the child or the environment in which they are cared for is not seen."

8.7   The National Children's Bureau both in its response and through membership of my reference group to this inquiry have raised similar concerns.

8.8   The National Association of Social Workers in Education (NASWE) is more equivocal in its response but recognises the difficulty for local authorities under existing guidance to exercise their duty of care.

---

20 NSPCC Response to DCSF Call for Evidence, April 2009

> *"The lack of regulation has made it very difficult for local authorities to exercise their duty of care to the child or young person concerned and may compromise a child's right to education. The legislation only makes it possible to consider the **education** on offer and this goes against all other aspects of their work with children which, encourages the consideration of a range of factors contributing to the ECM outcomes. EHE is not in itself a safeguarding issue although the failure to provide a satisfactory education (in any context) may seriously compromise a child's future opportunities. EHE removes the opportunity for what is a very efficient method for monitoring and surveillance through attendance at school. Consequently the issue of EHE has become conflated with safeguarding concerns which may exist regardless of the method by which a child receives education."*

8.9   Her Majesty's Chief Inspector (HMCI), in her submission, makes it clear that irrespective of the number of cases, change in regulation is necessary, furthermore that there is an unacceptable variation in the practice of local authorities and Local Safeguarding Children Boards (LSCB):

> *"Our experience from inspections of children's services and evaluations of serious case reviews is that there is variation across the country in how proactively local safeguarding children boards ensure these children are safeguarded. Some local child protection procedures address this robustly while others do not. Current DCSF guidelines for local authorities on elective home education place insufficient emphasis on safeguarding the welfare of children. In a small number of cases, our evaluation of serious case reviews has identified that a lack of oversight of children receiving home education contributed to a serious incident or the death of a child. Schools have an important responsibility to monitor children's safety and welfare but this safety net is missing for children educated at home. In addition, children who are educated at home may have less access to trusted adults who they can turn to if they are concerned about their home circumstances."*

8.10   Ofsted go on to report findings from a small study they conducted in 2008 into the effectiveness of local authority policies to manage the risks to children who are not attending school nor receiving education elsewhere.

> *"Some authorities expressed the view that securing adequate safeguarding would be easier if they had a clear right of access to family homes in the course of monitoring the suitability of home education. Some authorities reported that national organisations for home education were advising parents to deny access to officers from children's services who were attempting to establish the suitability of the provision. Ofsted is concerned that this advice may increase the risk of harm to some children. Children who are educated at home but are not known to the local authority may be more likely to be at risk. Local authorities are notified when children are removed from local authority school rolls. However, during the survey referred to above, five local authorities expressed concern that some independent schools in their area did not notify them when pupils were taken off roll."*[21]

8.11   Some of the concerns raised by the above are dealt with in earlier recommendations. However, in the light of the submission by HMCI and the other evidence, I recommend:

RECOMMENDATION 21

That the Children's Trust Board ensures that the Local Safeguarding Children Board (LSCB) reports to them on an annual basis with regard to the safeguarding provision and actions taken in relation to home educated children. This report shall also be sent to the National Safeguarding Delivery Unit. Such information should be categorised thereby avoiding current speculation with regard to the prevalence of child protection concerns amongst home educated children which may well be exaggerated. This information should contribute to and be contained within the National Annual Report.

8.12   To return to the two questions posed earlier. First, on the basis of local authority evidence and case studies presented, even acknowledging the variation between authorities, the number of children known to children's social care in some local authorities is disproportionately high relative to the size of their home educating population. Secondly, despite the small number of serious case reviews where home education was a feature, the consideration of these reviews and the data outlined above, suggests that those engaged in the support and monitoring of

---

21 DCSF is planning to implement Sir Roger Singleton's recent recommendation, as outlined in his report *'Keep our school safe'* (2009), to *"ensure that all independent and non-maintained schools are required to notify the LA when children of compulsory school age leave the roll, and to inform them of the destination where this is known to them"*. This change will be included the revision of the Independent School Standards that will take effect from September 2010.

home education should be alert to the potential additional risk to children. So saying is not to suggest that there is a causal or determining relationship, but simply an indication of the need for appropriately trained and knowledgeable personnel. To that end, I recommend:

RECOMMENDATION 22

That those responsible for monitoring and supporting home education, or commissioned so to do, are suitably qualified and experienced to discharge their duties and responsibilities set out in *Working Together to Safeguard Children*[22] to refer to social care services children who they believe to be in need of services or where there is reasonable cause to suspect that a child is suffering, or is likely to suffer, significant harm.

RECOMMENDATION 23

That local authority adult services and other agencies be required to inform those charged with the monitoring and support of home education of any properly evidenced concerns that they have of parents' or carers' ability to provide a suitable education irrespective of whether or not they are known to children's social care, on such grounds as:

- alcohol or drug abuse
- incidents of domestic violence
- previous offences against children

And in addition:

- anything else which may affect their ability to provide a suitable and efficient education.

This requirement should be considered in the Government's revision of *Working Together to Safeguard Children* Guidance.

8.13 Local authorities have a general duty, when carrying out functions in the education context, to safeguard and promote the welfare of children (section 175 Education Act 2002). Provision for the protection of children is contained in the Children Act 1989 and includes provision that local authorities have a duty to investigate where they have reasonable cause to suspect

22 DCSF (2006) *Working Together to Safeguard Children*, TSO, London.

that a child in their area is suffering or is likely to suffer significant harm. Whether a child may or may not have already come to the attention of the local authority because of safeguarding concerns, I believe it is of crucial importance in any registration scheme to give the local authority a discretion to prevent a child being electively home educated for safeguarding reasons. I therefore recommend:

RECOMMENDATION 24

That the DCSF make such change as is necessary to the legislative framework to enable local authorities to refuse registration on safeguarding grounds. In addition, local authorities should have the right to revoke registration should safeguarding concerns become apparent.

8.14 With regard to other specific groups within the remit of this inquiry I can find no evidence that elective home education is a particular factor in the removal of children to forced marriage, servitude or trafficking or for inappropriate abusive activities. Based on the limited evidence available, this view is supported by the Association of Chief Police Officers. That is not to say that there are not isolated cases of trafficking that have been brought to my attention.

8.15 The foregoing would confirm my view that had there been different regulations in place as proposed, they may well have had a mitigating effect without necessarily guaranteeing prevention. However, any regulation is only as effective as its transaction. To that end I believe it is important to hold local authorities to account, identify and disseminate good practice and ensure that in addition to the training proposed earlier, that local authority and other staff are adequately and properly trained in safeguarding procedures and requirements:

RECOMMENDATION 25

That the DCSF, in its revision of the National Indicator Set indicated in its response to the recent Laming Review, should incorporate an appropriate target relating to the safeguarding of children in elective home education.

RECOMMENDATION 26

DCSF should explore the potential for the Centre for Excellence and Outcomes in Children and Young People's Services (C4EO) and other organisations, to identify and disseminate good practice regarding support for home education.

RECOMMENDATION 27

It is recommended that the Children's Workforce Development Council and the National Safeguarding Delivery Unit include the needs of this group of officers in their consideration of national training needs.

9. Resources

9.1   Irrespective of any estimate of the number of children currently electively home educated, it is the case that should they return to school, they would immediately draw down the Age Weighted Pupil Unit (AWPU) value for a child of their age within that locality. At present no such funding attaches to them on becoming electively home educated. Local authorities meet their own costs and the cost of services provided are met from within their own resources – which in part accounts for the disparity of support provision.

9.2   I do not believe this to be fair or just. Yes, they (sometimes) and their parents have chosen to leave the schooling system but they remain in education and the state has a responsibility to use its best endeavours to promote their safety and achievement. To implement the registration scheme and meet the other requirements of this report, will undoubtedly require further resources. However, recognising that these resources are part of a complex arrangement between local authorities and the DCSF, I recommend:

RECOMMENDATION 28

That the DCSF and the Local Government Association determine within three months how to provide to local authorities sufficient resources to secure the recommendations in this report.

10. Issues Out of Scope of this Inquiry and the need for further research

10.1   Inevitably during the course of an inquiry, matters arise that require answers, yet either no answer is easily forthcoming, or in searching for it, one becomes aware that the evidence does not exist. In particular I am concerned by two issues. First, what constitutes 'autonomous' learning. Could it be, as many home educating parents have argued, it defies definition but provides the ultimate opportunity for children to develop at their own rate and expands their talents and aptitudes thought the pursuit of personal interest. Or, does it present a more serious concern for a quality of education that lacks pace, rigour and direction. I come to no conclusion but believe further research into the efficacy of autonomous learning is essential. Case law offers some insight:[23]

> "...in our judgment "education" demands at least an element of supervision; merely to allow a child to follow its own devices in the hope that it will acquire knowledge by imitation, experiment or experience in its own way and in its own good time is neither systematic nor instructive...such a course would not be education but, at best, child-minding."[23]

10.2   My second issue in part relates to the first. I am not convinced by the existing research studies on the outcomes for home educated children both in this country and elsewhere. Although some (but not all) studies have found that home educated children outperform schooled children on a range of indicators, the results may be attributable to parental characteristics (e.g. better educated parents with higher incomes). Some of the studies were also based on small samples and therefore the ability to generalise is limited. Some were based on self selecting, and therefore biased, samples. The diverse characteristics of home educated children make it difficult to generalise about their academic performance.

10.3   Furthermore, little is known about the collective outcomes for home educated children in terms of their qualifications and employment. Evidence offered to this inquiry on the proportion of home educated young people who are not in education, employment or training (NEET) was inconclusive. Again I believe further research is necessary that seeks information on progression to further and higher education and employment.

10.4   I suspect that should the recommendations in this report be accepted, these matters will demand and receive further attention.

---

23 Harrison and Harrison v Stevenson (1982) QB (DC) 729/81

11.Conclusion

11.1   International comparison suggests that of all countries with highly developed education systems, England is the most liberal in its approach to elective home education. Legislation from the 1930s banning elective home education still persists in Germany and most European countries require registration, whereas New Zealand demands that the "*person will be taught at least as regularly and as well as in registered school.*"[24] The majority of other countries also have processes for registration and the systematic monitoring of elective home education and require evidence of progress, often specifically in mathematics and reading.

11.2   The recommendations in this review do not go that far. I have sought to strike a balance between the rights of parents and the rights of the child, and offer, through registration and other recommendations, some assurance on the greater safety of a number of children.

11.3   I recognise that much of what is proposed can be implemented and achieved through advice and changes in guidance in due course. However I believe certain recommendations require immediate action. To that end, I urge the DCSF to respond to recommendations 1, 7, 23 and 24 as summarised in the next chapter, at the next available opportunity.

---

24   New Zealand Education Act 1989 No. 80 (as at 17 December 2008) Public Act, 21(1)(a)(i)

12. Summary of Recommendations

Recommendation 1

That the DCSF establishes a compulsory national registration scheme, locally administered, for all children of statutory school age, who are, or become, electively home educated.

- This scheme should be common to all local authorities.

- Registration should be renewed annually.

- Those who are registering for the first time should be visited by the appropriate local authority officer within one month of registration.

- Local authorities should ensure that all home educated children and young people already known to them are registered on the new scheme within one month of its inception and visited over the following twelve months, following the commencement of any new legislation.

- Provision should be made to allow registration at a local school, children's centre or other public building as determined by the local authority.

- When parents are thinking of deregistering their child/children from school to home educate, schools should retain such pupils on roll for a period of 20 school days so that should there be a change in circumstances, the child could be readmitted to the school. This period would also allow for the resolution of such difficulties that may have prompted the decision to remove the child from school.

- National guidance should be issued on the requirements of registration and be made available online and at appropriate public buildings. Such guidance must include a clear statement of the statutory basis of elective home education and the rights and responsibilities of parents.

- At the time of registration parents/carers/guardians must provide a clear statement of their educational approach, intent and desired/planned outcomes for the child over the following twelve months.

- Guidance should be issued to support parents in this task with an opportunity to meet local authority officers to discuss the planned approach to home education and develop the plan before it is finalised. The plan should be finalised within eight weeks of first registration.

- As well as written guidance, support should encompass advice from a range of advisers and organisations, including schools. Schools should regard this support as a part of their commitment to extended schooling.

- Where a child is removed from a school roll to be home educated, the school must provide to the appropriate officer of the local authority a record of the child's achievement to date and expected achievement, within 20 school days of the registration, together with any other school records.

- Local authorities must ensure that there are mechanisms/systems in place to record and review registrations annually.

Recommendation 2

That the DCSF review the current statutory definition of what constitutes a "suitable" and "efficient" education in the light of the Rose review of the primary curriculum, and other changes to curriculum assessment and definition throughout statutory school age. Such a review should take account of the five Every Child Matters outcomes determined by the 2004 Children Act, should not be overly prescriptive but be sufficiently defined to secure a broad, balanced, relevant and differentiated curriculum that would allow children and young people educated at home to have sufficient information to enable them to expand their talents and make choices about likely careers. The outcome of this review should further inform guidance on registration.

Home educators should be engaged in this process.

Recommendation 3

That all local authorities analyse the reasons why parents or carers chose elective home education and report those findings to the Children's Trust Board, ensuring that this analysis contributes to the debate that determines the Children and Young People's Plan.

Recommendation 4

That the local authority should establish a Consultative Forum for home educating parents to secure their views and representative opinion. Such a body could be constituted as a sub-group of the Children's Trust with a role in supporting the development of the Children's Trust, and the intentions of the local authority with regard to elective home education.

Recommendation 5

That the DCSF should bring forward proposals requiring all local authorities to report to the Children's Trust Board making clear how it intends to monitor and support children and young people being educated at home, in accord with Recommendation 1.

Recommendation 6

That local authorities should where appropriate commission the monitoring and support of home education through the local Children's Trust Board, thereby securing a multidisciplinary approach and the likely use of expertise from other agencies and organisations including the voluntary sector.

Recommendation 7

The DCSF should bring forward proposals to change the current regulatory and statutory basis to ensure that in monitoring the efficiency and suitability of elective home education:

- That designated local authority officers should:
  - have the right of access to the home;
  - have the right to speak with each child alone if deemed appropriate or, if a child is particularly vulnerable or has particular communication needs, in the company of a trusted person who is not the home educator or the parent/carer.

In so doing, officers will be able to satisfy themselves that the child is safe and well.

- That a requirement is placed upon local authorities to secure the monitoring of the effectiveness of elective home education as determined in Recommendation 1.
- That parents be required to allow the child through exhibition or other means to demonstrate both attainment and progress in accord with the statement of intent lodged at the time of registration.

Recommendation 8

That reasonable warning of intended visit and invitation to exhibit should be given to home educators, parents and carers, not less than two weeks in advance. A written report of each visit must be filed within 21 days and copied to the home educating parent and child. A suitable process for factual correction and challenge to the content must be in place and made known to all parties.

Recommendation 9

That all local authority officers and others engaged in the monitoring and support of elective home education must be suitably trained. This training must include awareness of safeguarding issues and a full understanding of the essential difference, variation and diversity in home education practice, as compared to schools. Wherever possible and appropriate, representatives of the home educating community should be involved in the development and/or provision of such training. It is recommended that all officers be trained in the use of the Common Assessment Framework.

Recommendation 10

That all local authorities should offer a menu of support to home educating families in accord with the requirements placed upon them by the power of wellbeing, extended schools and community engagement and other legislation. To that end local authorities must provide support for home educating children and young people to find appropriate examination centres and provide entries free to all home educated candidates who have demonstrated sufficiently their preparedness through routine monitoring, for all DCSF funded qualifications.

Recommendation 11

That in addition to Recommendation 10 above, local authorities should, in collaboration with schools and colleges:

- Extend and make available the opportunities of flexi-schooling.
- Extend access to school libraries, sports facilities, school visits, specialist facilities and key stage assessment.
- Provide access to specialist music tuition on the same cost basis.
- Provide access to work experience.
- Provide access to post 14 vocational opportunities.
- Signpost to third sector support where they have specialist experience and knowledge, for example, provision for bullied children.

Recommendation 12

- BECTA considers the needs of the home educating community in the national roll out of the home access initiative
- That local authorities consider what support and access to ICT facilities could be given to home educating children and young people through the existing school networks and the use of school based materials
- That the QCA should consider the use of ICT in the testing and exam process with regard to its impact on home educated children and young

Recommendation 13

That local authority provision in regard to elective home education is brought into the scope of Ofsted's assessment of children's services within the Comprehensive Area Assessment through information included in the National Indicator Set (Recommendation 25), the annual LSCB report (Recommendation 21) and any other relevant information available to inspectors.

Recommendation 14

That the DCSF require all local authorities to make an annual return to the Children's Trust Board regarding the number of electively home educated children and young people and the number of School Attendance Orders and Education Supervision Orders as defined in the 1996 Education Act, issued to home educated children and young people.

Recommendation 15

That the DCSF take such action as necessary to prevent schools or local authorities advising parents to consider home education to prevent permanent exclusion or using such a mechanism to deal with educational or behavioural issues.

Recommendation 16

That the DCSF bring forward proposals to give local authorities power of direction with regard to school places for children and young people returning to school from home education above planned admission limits in circumstances where it is quite clear that the needs of the child or young person could not be met without this direction.

Recommendation 17

That the Ofsted review of SEN provision give due consideration to home educated children with special educational needs and make specific reference to the support of those children.

Recommendation 18

That the DCSF should reinforce in guidance to local authorities the requirement to exercise their statutory duty to assure themselves that education is suitable and meets the child's special educational needs. They should regard the move to home education as a trigger to conduct a review and satisfy themselves that the potentially changed complexity of education provided at home, still constitutes a suitable education. The statement should then be revised accordingly to set out that the parent has made their own arrangements under section 7 of the Education Act 1996.

In the wake of the Ofsted review, changes to the SEN framework and legislation may be required.

Recommendation 19

That the statutory review of statements of SEN in accord with Recommendation 18 above be considered as fulfilling the function of mandatory annual review of elective home education recommended previously.

Recommendation 20

When a child or young person without a statement of special educational needs has been in receipt of School Action Plus support, local authorities and other agencies should give due consideration to whether that support should continue once the child is educated at home – irrespective of whether or not such consideration requires a new commissioning of service.

Recommendation 21

That the Children's Trust Board ensures that the Local Safeguarding Children Board (LSCB) reports to them on an annual basis with regard to the safeguarding provision and actions taken in relation to home educated children. This report shall also be sent to the National Safeguarding Delivery Unit. Such information should be categorised thereby avoiding current speculation with regard to the prevalence of child protection concerns amongst home educated children which may well be exaggerated. This information should contribute to and be contained within the National Annual Report.

Recommendation 22

That those responsible for monitoring and supporting home education, or commissioned so to do, are suitably qualified and experienced to discharge their duties and responsibilities set out in *Working Together to Safeguard Children* to refer to social care services children who they believe to be in need of services or where there is reasonable cause to suspect that a child is suffering, or is likely to suffer, significant harm.

Recommendation 23

That local authority adult services and other agencies be required to inform those charged with the monitoring and support of home education of any properly evidenced concerns that they have of parents' or carers' ability to provide a suitable education irrespective of whether or not they are known to children's social care, on such grounds as

- alcohol or drug abuse

- incidents of domestic violence

- previous offences against children

And in addition:

- anything else which may affect their ability to provide a suitable and efficient education

This requirement should be considered in the Government's revision of *Working Together to Safeguard Children* Guidance.

Recommendation 24

That the DCSF make such change as is necessary to the legislative framework to enable local authorities to refuse registration on safeguarding grounds. In addition local authorities should have the right to revoke registration should safeguarding concerns become apparent.

Recommendation 25

That the DCSF, in its revision of the National Indicator Set indicated in its response to the recent Laming Review, should incorporate an appropriate target relating to the safeguarding of children in elective home education.

Recommendation 26

DCSF should explore the potential for Centre for Excellence and Outcomes in Children and Young People's Services (C4EO) and other organisations, to identify and disseminate good practice regarding support for home education.

Recommendation 27

It is recommended that the Children's Workforce Development Council and the National Safeguarding Delivery Unit include the needs of this group of officers in their consideration of national training needs.

Recommendation 28

That the DCSF and the Local Government Association determine within three months how to provide to local authorities sufficient resources to secure the recommendations in this report.

Annex A – Review Terms of Reference

Background and Rationale

The Department is committed to ensuring that systems for keeping children safe, and ensuring that they receive a suitable education, are as robust as possible. An independent review of home education is part of this continuing commitment.

Parents have a well established right to educate their children at home and Government respects that right. There are no plans to change that position.

However, where local authorities have concerns about the safety and welfare, or education, of a home educated child, effective systems must be in place to deal with those concerns. The review will assess the effectiveness of current arrangements and will, if necessary, make recommendations for improvements.

Terms of reference

The review of home education will investigate:

- The barriers to local authorities and other public agencies in carrying out their responsibilities for safeguarding home educated children and advise on improvements to ensure that the five Every Child Matters outcomes are being met for home educated children;

- The extent to which claims of home education could be used as a 'cover' for child abuse such as neglect, forced marriage, sexual exploitation or domestic servitude and advise on measures to prevent this;

- Whether local authorities are providing the right type, level and balance of support to home educating families to ensure they are undertaking their duties to provide a suitable full time education to their children;

- Whether any changes to the current regime for monitoring the standard of home education are needed to support the work of parents, local authorities and other partners in ensuring all children achieve the Every Child Matters outcomes.

Timing

The review will be conducted over 4 months, starting in January 2009 and concluding in April 2009 with a published report in May 2009. Ministers will then consider whether any further work is required on any aspect of home education, on the basis of the findings contained in the review report.

Scope

The Review will focus on practice in England but may consider relevant material from the devolved administrations within the UK and elsewhere.

Review methodology

The review will be led by Graham Badman, former Managing Director, Children, Families and Education in Kent. It will:

- Map existing practice and consider the effectiveness of different practice – including identifying best practice – in England and elsewhere in monitoring home education from an Every Child Matters perspective;

- Identify what evidence there is that claims of home education are, or could be, used as a 'cover' for child abuse under current monitoring practice;

- Consider evidence of the effectiveness of current monitoring practice contained in Serious Case Reviews, Joint Area Reviews and other relevant inspections and reviews;

- Seek evidence on how the systems operate in practice from key stakeholders including home education groups, home educating families, local authorities and children's charities;

- Identify areas for improvement and make recommendations for any changes to strengthen current arrangements.

The review will gather views and evidence through a literature review, a review of the law and guidance and a series of interviews with key stakeholders representing the range of interests. It will consider how effectively arrangements are currently operating, focusing on the operation of systems and procedures and not on individual cases. The review team will contact key stakeholders and invite submissions. Other stakeholders who wish to contribute can do so via a questionnaire available at www.dcsf.gov.uk/consultations.

The review will also consider the views of stakeholders gathered as part of the recent public consultation on the statutory guidance on children not receiving a suitable education.

Annex B – List of Consultees

Association of Chief Police Officers

Association of Directors of Children's Services

Association of Education Welfare Managers

Autism in Mind

Bedfordshire County Council

Birmingham City Council

British Dyslexia Association

Cheshire County Council

Professor James Conroy

Department of Health

Derbyshire County Council

Education Otherwise

Family Education Trust

Forced Marriage Unit, Foreign and Commonwealth Office

Gloucestershire County Council

Home Education Advisory Service

Home Education Research Association

Independent Panel for Special Educational Advice (IPSEA)

Islamic Home Schooling Advisory Network

Arthur Ivatts

Leicestershire County Council

Local Government Association

National Association of Social Workers in Education

National Autism Society

NCB

North Yorkshire County Council

NSPCC

Ofsted

Dr Paula Rothermel

Alison Sauer, Sauer Consulting

Professor Alan Thomas

Staffordshire County Council

Wandsworth Council

West Sussex County Council

Wolverhampton Council

Worcestershire County Council

And numerous home educating parents and children.

Annex C – Public call for evidence questionnaire

Thank you for taking the time to complete this questionnaire about home education.

The Government is committed to ensuring that systems for keeping children safe, and ensuring that they receive a suitable education, are as robust as possible. An independent review of home education is part of this continuing commitment. The Review will look in particular at if and how far home educated children have access to the five Every Child Matters outcomes (see www.everychildmatters.gov.uk for more information).

These outcomes are:

- Be healthy
- Stay safe
- Enjoy and achieve
- Make a positive contribution
- Achieve economic wellbeing

The full terms of reference for the review are available on-line at www.everychildmatters.gov.uk/ete/homeeducation

The Secretary of State for Children, Schools and Families has asked Graham Badman CBE, to lead this independent review. Mr Badman is gathering evidence about current working arrangements from a range of key stakeholders such as home educating families and home educated children; local authority staff responsible for ensuring the safety, wellbeing and education of children and young people; and other organisations that represent children, young people and families, such as children's charities.

As part of that process, we would be very interested to hear your responses to the questions below.

Please return your completed questionnaire by **Friday 20th February 2009** to homeeducation.review@dcsf.gsi.gov.uk

Thank you for taking time to respond to these questions.

Section One – About You

1. Please specify in what capacity you are responding to this questionnaire.

	Please tick	Please provide more information if you wish
A home educating parent		
A home educated child		
Working in local authority with responsibility for home educated children		
Working in local authority with other responsibilities		
Working with children or families in another capacity (e.g. third sector)		
Member of the general public		
Other organisation/capacity *(please specify)*		

Section Two –Questions

2. Do you think the current system for safeguarding children who are educated at home is adequate?

Yes   ☐   Why do you think that?

```
┌─────────────────────────────────────────────────────────┐
│                                                         │
│                                                         │
│                                                         │
│                                                         │
│                                                         │
└─────────────────────────────────────────────────────────┘
```

No   ☐   Why do you think that?

```
┌─────────────────────────────────────────────────────────┐
│                                                         │
│                                                         │
│                                                         │
│                                                         │
│                                                         │
└─────────────────────────────────────────────────────────┘
```

Don't know   ☐

3. Do you think that home educated children are able to achieve the five Every Child Matters outcomes?

Yes   ☐   Please say why for each of the five outcomes.

Be healthy

Stay safe

Enjoy and achieve

Make a positive contribution

Achieve economic well-being

No ☐ Please say why for each of the five outcomes.

Be healthy

Stay safe

Enjoy and achieve

Make a positive contribution

Achieve economic well-being

4. Do you think that Government and local authorities have an obligation to ensure that all children in this country are able to achieve the five outcomes?

Yes ☐ How do you think Government should ensure this?

```



```

No ☐ Why do you think that?

```



```

Don't know ☐

5. Do you think there should be any changes made to the current system for supporting home educating families?

Yes ☐ What should they be?

```



```

No ☐   Why do you think that?

```
┌─────────────────────────────────────────────────────────────────┐
│                                                                   │
│                                                                   │
│                                                                   │
│                                                                   │
│                                                                   │
└─────────────────────────────────────────────────────────────────┘
```

Don't know ☐

6. Do you think there should be any changes made to the current system for monitoring home educating families?

Yes ☐   What should they be?

```
┌─────────────────────────────────────────────────────────────────┐
│                                                                   │
│                                                                   │
│                                                                   │
│                                                                   │
│                                                                   │
└─────────────────────────────────────────────────────────────────┘
```

No ☐   Why do you think that?

```
┌─────────────────────────────────────────────────────────────────┐
│                                                                   │
│                                                                   │
│                                                                   │
│                                                                   │
│                                                                   │
└─────────────────────────────────────────────────────────────────┘
```

Don't know ☐

7. Some people have expressed concern that home education could be used as a cover for child abuse, forced marriage, domestic servitude or other forms of child neglect. What do you think Government should do to ensure this cannot happen again?

Thank you for taking time to respond to these questions.

Please return your completed questionnaire, by **Friday 20th February 2009**, to homeeducation.review@dcsf.gsi.gov.uk

Annex D – Questionnaire to local authorities

Independent Review of Home Education in England

Thank you for taking the time to complete this questionnaire about processes for supporting and monitoring home education. You may find it helpful to read through the questionnaire before attempting to complete it. **Completion of the questionnaire is entirely voluntary.** Responses will be completely confidential and used only for the purposes of the independent review.

The Government is committed to ensuring that systems for keeping children safe are as robust as possible. As part of this continuing commitment, an independent review of home education will assess whether the right systems are in place for ensuring that home educated children have access to the five Every Child Matters outcomes. This includes whether Government should do more to support local authorities in discharging their duties in relation to home educated children. The full terms of reference for the review are available on-line at www.everychildmatters.gov.uk/ete/homeeducation

As organisations responsible for ensuring the safety, wellbeing and education of children and young people in your localities, we very much value your input into this review.

Please note, the Director of Children's Services and Lead Member for Children and Young People are asked to sign off the response to this questionnaire before submitting it.

Please return your completed questionnaire by **Friday 6 February** to homeeducation.review@dcsf.gsi.gov.uk

Or by post to:

Elizabeth Green
Home Education Review
DCSF
Level 2
Sanctuary Buildings
Great Smith Street
London SW1P 3BT

Thank you for taking time to respond to these questions.

Section One – About your local authority

Name of LA	
Tel. No of main contact	
E-mail of main contact	

Would you be willing to take part in the next phase of the research in March (including in-depth interviews with key personnel in your organisation)?	Yes/No

1. Who is involved in supporting and monitoring home educated children within the local authority and other agencies?

Team with main responsibility –	
List all teams/professionals involved	
Support	Monitoring
Describe how you ensure collaboration and communication between these teams/individuals	

Section Two – Data and Tracking

2. How many children are currently home educated in your local authority?

Phase	Registered with LA	Non-registered children
Primary age		
Secondary age		
Total		

3. Are these figures accurate or based on estimates?

Accurate ☐

> *Where do you get this data from?*
>
>
>
>
> *How do you know the data are accurate?*

Estimate ☐

> *What data have you used to arrive at this figure? (List all sources)*

4. How confident are you in the accuracy of this data?

Very confident ☐   Fairly confident ☐   Don't know ☐

Not very confident ☐   Not at all confident ☐

5. How often does the local authority get updated data?

> *List frequency for each source separately*

6. Thinking about your home educated population, what proportions have the following characteristics? *Please say whether these figures are based on estimates or accurate data.*

Characteristic	Proportion	*Delete as appropriate*
Statement for SEN		Estimate/accurate
Non-statemented SEN		Estimate/accurate
Gypsy, Roma, Traveller heritage		Estimate/accurate
Other BME Group *(please state below)*		Estimate/accurate
•		Estimate/accurate
•		Estimate/accurate
•		Estimate/accurate

7. Do you believe the local authority knows about all the home educated children in your area?

Yes, we are confident we know about all home educated children in the area ☐

We think we know about the vast majority of home educated children in the area ☐

We probably do not know about a fair number of home educated children in the area ☐

We probably do not know about a significant proportion of home educated children in the area ☐

8. Do you think that you will be better able to track children in your area in the near future?
e.g. planned changes to your own systems, ContactPoint, other system improvements?

Yes ☐

Why do you think that?

No ☐

Why do you think that?

Don't know ☐

Section Three – Supporting Home Educating Families

9. How does the local authority ensure families know about their rights and responsibilities in relation to home education?

List all approaches used

10. What support does your local authority provide to home educating families?

List all forms of support offered

11. How does the local authority let families know about the services provided to support them in home educating their children?

List all approaches used

Section Four – Assessment and Monitoring

12. Following the initial assessment visit, are further monitoring visits made to a home educated child?

Yes ☐   No ☐   Don't know ☐

12a. If yes, how often, on average, are these carried out?

More than twice a year ☐   How often? _____

Twice a year ☐   Once a year ☐

Less than once a year ☐

Additional comments

13. On average, how often is the child seen when a visit is made?

Always, at each visit ☐   Usually, but not always ☐

Sometimes ☐   Never ☐

Depends on the child/circumstances ☐   *Please describe*

14. If the child is seen, where is s/he usually seen?

In the home ☐   At the home, but do not go inside ☐

Another venue ☐   Please specifiy _____

Depends on the child/circumstances ☐

Please describe

15. If you are not permitted access to a child, is any further action taken?

Yes ☐   No ☐   Don't know ☐

15a.   If yes, what further steps are taken?

Please describe

16. How is the 'suitability' of the education provided to the child assessed?

Please describe

17. Is the local authority clear about what the definition of a 'suitable education' is?

Yes ☐

> *Why is that?*

No ☐

> *Why is that?*

18. **Does the local authority have systems in place to track the educational progress of home educated children?**

Yes ☐ No ☐ Don't know ☐

> *If yes, please describe the system*

19. **Of the home educated children in your area of whom you have knowledge, what proportion in your estimation are receiving a suitable, full time (20hrs a week) education?**

> *Please describe*

20. Does the local authority take any further steps if a home educated child's education was found to be unsuitable or not full time?

Yes ☐   No ☐   Don't know ☐

20a. If yes, what steps are then taken?

Please describe

21. Does the local authority face any challenges in assessing whether home educated children receive a suitable education?

Yes ☐   No ☐   Don't know ☐

If yes, please describe challenges and what you think could be done to overcome these

22. Thinking about your local area, in the last five years[25], how many cases have you come across that use the premise of home education as a 'cover' for child abuse, forced marriage or other aspects of child neglect?

Please specify number[26] _____

Additional comments
Please include the number of Serious Case Reviews you know about that have a home education element

---

25 Since January 2003
26 NB – this data will not be aggregated or used in any other way. This data will provide an overall sense of the scale of this issue

23. Do you think the current system for safeguarding children who are educated at home is adequate?

Yes ☐ *Why do you think that?*

> (blank text box)

No ☐ *Why do you think that?*

> (blank text box)

Don't know ☐

24. Do you think that home educated children in your local authority are able to achieve the five Every Child Matters outcomes?

Yes ☐ Please say why for each of the five outcomes.

Be healthy
Stay safe
Enjoy and achieve

Make a positive contribution

Achieve economic well-being

No ☐   Please say why for each of the five outcomes.

Be healthy

Stay safe

Enjoy and achieve

Make a positive contribution

Achieve economic well-being

25. Do you think there should be any changes made to the current system for supporting home educated families?

Yes ☐ *What should they be?*

```



```

No ☐ *Why do you think that?*

```



```

Don't know ☐

26. Do you think there should be any changes made to the current system for monitoring home educating families and ensuring that home educated children are able to achieve the five outcomes?

Yes ☐ *What should they be?*

```



```

No ☐   *Why do you think that?*

Don't know ☐

Thank you for taking time to respond to these questions.

Please return your completed questionnaire, by **Friday 6 February** to homeeducation.review@dcsf. gsi.gov.uk or by post to the address on page one. If you are returning the questionnaire electronically, please add the name of the DCS and Lead Member in the signature box.

Declaration

I agree that the information supplied in this questionnaire is a true reflection of practice in this local authority.

Signed _____   Date _____
Director of Children's Services

Signed _____   Date _____
Lead Member for Children

The information you have provided may be subject to the Freedom of Information Act 2000. This does not necessarily mean that your response can be made available to the public as there are exemptions relating to information provided in confidence and information to which the Data Protection Act 1998 applies. You may request confidentiality by ticking the box provided, but you should note that this may not exclude the public right of access.

Please tick if you want to keep your response confidential ☐

Annex E – Legislative framework

1. Children's rights

1.1 The United Nations Convention on the Rights of the Child (UNCRC) is an international human rights treaty that grants all children and young people (aged 17 and under) a comprehensive set of rights. It came into force in the UK on 15 January 1992. When a country ratifies the convention it agrees to do everything it can to implement it.

1.2 The convention gives children and young people over forty substantive rights which include the right to express their views freely, the right to be heard in any legal or administrative matters that affect them and the right to seek, receive and impart information and ideas (Articles 12 and 13). It also includes the right to an education (Article 28).

1.3 Section 53 of the 2004 Children Act sets out the duty on local authorities to, where reasonably practicable, take into account the child's wishes and feelings with regard to the provision of services.

1.4 Local authorities must ensure that functions conferred on them in their capacity as a local education authority are exercised with a view to safeguarding and promoting the welfare of children. Duties under the Children Act 1989 impose a requirement on local authorities to safeguard and promote the welfare of children in need in their area and to make enquiries and take appropriate steps where there are concerns about a child's welfare.[27]

2. Parent's rights, responsibilities and duties

2.1 The Human Rights Act 1998 came into effect on 2 October 2000. The purpose of the Act is to give effect to the rights and freedoms guaranteed under the European Convention on Human Rights ("the Convention"). Convention rights are enforceable through domestic courts, legislation should be interpreted so far as possible so as to be compatible with the convention and it is unlawful for public authorities to act in a way which is incompatible with a Convention right. Article 2 Protocol 1 of the Convention provides:

> *"No person shall be denied the right to education. In the exercise of any functions which it assumes in relation to education and to teaching, the State shall respect the right of parents to ensure such education and teaching is in conformity with their own religious and philosophical convictions."*

---

27 Sections 17 and 47 of the Children Act 1989

2.2   Education is therefore a fundamental right and can be provided at school "or otherwise".[28] The responsibility for the provision of a child's education rests with their parents who also have a duty to ensure that any education provided is 'efficient', 'full time' and 'suitable'. This is set out in Section 7 of the Education Act 1996 which provides that:

> "The parent of every child of compulsory school age shall cause him to receive efficient full-time education suitable –
> (a)   to his age, ability and aptitude, and
> (b)   to any special educational needs he may have, either by regular attendance at school or otherwise."

2.3   The terms "efficient" and "suitable" education are not defined in law although case law[29] has broadly described an "efficient" education as one that "achieves that which it sets out to achieve". A "suitable" education is one that:

> "primarily equips a child for life within the community of which he is a member, rather than the way of life in the country as a whole, as long as it does not foreclose the child's options in later years to adopt some other form of life if he wishes to do so".

2.4   Parents may decide to educate their child at home and they can do this at any time during statutory school age. Should parents decide to home educate from the start of statutory school age, they can do so and do not have to inform anyone e.g. the local authority. If the child was previously on a maintained school or independent school roll, parents must officially deregister from the school which is then obliged to inform the local authority.[30]

3.   Local authorities' responsibilities

3.1   Local authorities have a statutory duty to make arrangements to enable them to establish the identities, "so far as it is possible to do so", of children in their area who are not receiving a suitable education.[31] The duty applies in relation to children of statutory school age who are not on a school roll, and who are not receiving a suitable education otherwise than being at school (for example, at home, privately, or in alternative provision).

---

28 Section 7 Education Act 1996
29 Mr Justice Woolf in the case of R v Secretary of State for Education and Science, ex parte Talmud Torah Machzikei Hadass School Trust (12 April 1985)
30 Education (Pupil Registration) (England) Regulations 2006 (SI 2006/1751)
31 Section 436A of the Education Act 1996, inserted by the Education and Inspections Act 2006

3.2   Under Section 437(1) of the Education Act 1996, local authorities shall intervene if it appears that parents are not providing a suitable education.

> *"If it appears to a local education authority that a child of compulsory school age in their area is not receiving suitable education, either by regular attendance at school or otherwise, they shall serve a notice in writing on the parent requiring him to satisfy them within the period specified in the notice that the child is receiving such education."*

3.3   Guidance states that *"local authorities need to make arrangements which will as far as possible enable them to determine whether any children who are not pupils at schools, such as those being educated at home, are receiving suitable education. In order to do this local authorities should make inquiries with parents educating children at home about the educational provision being made for them".*[32] Parents are under no duty to respond to such enquiries, but case law provides that "*it would be sensible for them to do so*".[33]

3.4   Local authorities can apply to serve a School Attendance Order if after all reasonable steps have been taken, they are not satisfied that a suitable education is being provided. At any stage following the issue of the Order, parents may present evidence to the local authority that they are now providing an appropriate education and apply to have the Order revoked.[34]

3.5   Local authorities also have a duty to safeguard and promote the welfare of children.[35] This section states:

> *"A local education authority shall make arrangements for ensuring that the functions conferred upon them in their capacity as a local education authority are exercised with a view to safeguarding and promoting the welfare of children."*

This duty does not give local authorities powers to see children for the purposes of monitoring the provision of home education.

---

32 *Revised statutory guidance for local authorities in England to identify children not receiving a suitable education*, DCSF, January 2009; section 87

33 *Philips v Brown* (unreported transcript 424/78 QB (DC)) 20 June 1980

34 Detailed information about school attendance orders is contained in *Ensuring Regular School Attendance* paragraphs 6 to 16

35 Under section 175(1) of the Education Act 2002

3.6 Where a child who has a statement of special educational needs and is on the roll of a special school the child's name may not be removed from the register of that school without the local authority's consent. Consent may not unreasonably be withheld. If a child who has a statement of SEN is educated at home it remains the duty of the local authority to ensure that the child's needs are met. The statement must remain in place and it is the local authority's statutory duty to undertake an annual review of special educational needs. This review includes assessing whether the statement is still appropriate, requires amendment or might cease to be maintained. If parents' arrangements are suitable then the local authority is relieved of its duty to arrange the provision specified in the statement.

Annex F – Expert Reference Group

Sue Berelowitz, Deputy Children's Commissioner/Chief Executive, 11 MILLION.

Professor James Conroy, Dean of Faculty of Education, University of Glasgow.

Paul Ennals, Chief Executive/Jacqui Newvell, Policy Officer, NCB.

Stephen Hart, Her Majesty's Inspector, Ofsted.

Professor Stephen Heppell, University of Bournemouth, Chair of Trustees, The Inclusion Trust.

Jean Humphrys, Director, Early Years Development, Ofsted.

Professor Edward Melhuish, Birkbeck, University of London.

Delroy Pommell, Director, London and the South East, Barnardos.

Beth Reid, National Autistic Society.

Professor June Statham, Institute of Education, University of London.

Printed in the UK for The Stationery Office Limited
on behalf of the Controller of Her Majesty's Stationery Office
ID6173620   06/09

Printed on Paper containing 75% recycled fibre content minimum